D0841452

Word Dances

A Collection of Verses and Thoughts
about Ballroom Dancing

Joseph Michael Sepesy

The most beautiful reason for dancing ... is in your arms.

Copyright © 2011, 2014 Joseph Michael Sepesy.

All rights reserved. No part of this book may be reproduced, stored, or transmitted by any means—whether auditory, graphic, mechanical, or electronic—without written permission of both publisher and author, except in the case of brief excerpts used in critical articles and reviews. Unauthorized reproduction of any part of this work is illegal and is punishable by law.

ISBN: 978-1-312-39672-2 (sc)
ISBN: 978-1-4834-1929-9 (e)

Library of Congress Control Number: 2014917874

Because of the dynamic nature of the Internet, any web addresses or links contained in this book may have changed since publication and may no longer be valid. The views expressed in this work are solely those of the author and do not necessarily reflect the views of the publisher, and the publisher hereby disclaims any responsibility for them.

Any people depicted in stock imagery provided by Thinkstock are models, and such images are being used for illustrative purposes only. Certain stock imagery © Thinkstock.

Lulu Publishing Services rev. date: 10/21/2014

R0443416480

This book is dedicated to my dear friend ... my inspiration, my dance teacher, Lynda McPhail.

Contents

Part 3

Dances and the Heart

Part 4

Dance Miscellanea

Epilogue

Acknowledgment

My dance teacher, Lynda McPhail, calls her dance studio A Time to Dance, but it is much more than a place where dance instruction occurs. A Time to Dance represents the talent and caring, the perseverance and dedication, of one of the most unique, gifted, and special ladies I have ever known. The following verse is for Lynda.

A Time to Dance

Her years have been defined by displays of courage, survival, and triumph. She has endured life's pains and suffering, its fears and cruelties. And throughout all but two of her years, she has danced with a beautiful passion ... danced all genres, with all their flavors.

Hers has been a time of strength.

> *To everything there is a season, and a time to every purpose under the heaven.*

She has learned and continues to learn, teach, and practices to perfect her craft. Her knowledge is great, and she is tested continually. She has honored her profession, excelling and loving her art ... and still hopes and dreams of many, many more dances to come.

Hers has been a time of accomplishment.

> *A time to be born, and a time to die; a time to plant, and a time to pluck up that which is planted.*

> *A time to kill and a time to heal; a time to break down, and a time to build up.*

She sees the ability in others and cultivates it, teaching, guiding, persuading ... and at times, working miracles. With their progress comes her satisfaction, her thrills, and that cannot be diminished. She gives of herself, her time and talent so that all may have ... their own times to dance.

Hers is a time of teaching.

> *A time to weep and a time to laugh; a time to mourn and a time to dance.*

A time to cast away stones, and a time to gather stones together; a time to embrace and a time to refrain from embracing.

She gives and receives gifts of the heart, touches and comforts spirits. She cares, speaks words of encouragement, and shows understanding. In turn, those assured and inspired have shown desire and endeavored to be her best ... and have pledged their loyalty.

Hers is a time of sharing.

A time to get and a time to lose; a time to keep and a time to cast away.

A time to rend, and a time to sew; a time to keep silence and a time to speak.

She has heard the applause and celebrated successes, those of her students and those that are personal. In a lifetime of dance, she has felt its power and rejoiced every day of every season ... and offered the same. Having accepted the offer, her students stand at her side ... and strive.

Hers has been a time of pride.

A time to love and a time to hate; a time of war and a time of peace.

Ecclesiastes 3:4

She represents the best of music and movement, with dances beyond the physical ... achieving dances of the spirit and emotions. She has been blessed and shares her blessings. She transcends her art, making differences in the world of dance and the lives of her students ... and lives her calling.

Hers has been and is ... hers will always be ... *a time to dance.*

Preface

I am a musical person. In 1956, when I was six years old, my dad put a guitar in my hands. He and Mom paid for music lessons for the next ten years. My brothers and I formed a band, and we performed at hundreds of weddings and dances in our home area. I danced in the freestyle way to the rock 'n' roll of the sixties and seventies but had no formal instruction ... and no interest in the *art* of dancing. Ballroom dancing was something foreign to me and remained so for the first fifty-nine years of my life. When *Dancing with the Stars* began its run on television, I enjoyed it from afar ... as a spectator.

Shortly after Thanksgiving of 2009, I was challenged to do something new in my life, something that would change the way I dealt with my post-traumatic stress disorder (PTSD), the result of three, combat tours of duty in Vietnam as a US Army helicopter pilot. I chose ballroom dancing, something that had interested me and entertained me for quite some time. Lynda McPhail, was recommended as an instructor.

I contacted Lynda and set up a private lesson. A week later, I limped across a dance floor with notebook and music CDs in hand—audaciousness she never lets me forget. But in my own defense, I knew exactly what I wanted to learn, so I brought some of my favorite tunes for the lesson. I didn't know how my injured spine, balance problem, and nerve-damaged feet would affect my ability to dance.

We started with swing, and in ten minutes, I was enjoying music like never before. I was dancing, really dancing. We tried a rumba next, and I was hooked. I was falling in love with dancing ... ballroom dancing. That life-altering day was December 2, 2009.

I enjoy Latin rhythms and melodies the most, so my third choice was the tango, coincidentally, Lynda's favorite dance. However, learning the tango is more difficult and really not for an absolute novice. But my enthusiasm and determination became apparent, and with Lynda's approval, swing, rumba, and the tango became our focus. Within four weeks, I attended another private lesson, attended social dances twice, and began taking Lynda's group lessons.

Soon, I was racking up as many as five lessons per week and attending numerous dances in the local area. In six months, I had performed a tango with Lynda at a dance event; what a confidence boost. All the while our friendship grew stronger and stronger.

Because of dance, I have become physically stronger, lost twenty-five pounds, improved my posture and carriage, diminished my chronic pain, and bolstered my self-confidence. I still limp but not when dancing, something doctors are unable to explain. I'll never overcome my PTSD, but I have learned how to deal with it in ways that it doesn't interfere with my life as much as it once did. To a large degree, dancing has set me free and tamed the demons of traumas from my past. Furthermore, Lynda has worked miracles, adjusting and compensating, helping me to overcome my troublesome and limiting physical conditions.

In the span of four years, I have learned twelve dances and performed the waltz, East and West Coast swings, tango, bolero, and rumba at public events. I now dance as much as five times a week, including lessons and social dancing. With the understanding, support, and encouragement of dozens of members of my dance community, I continue to improve … I dance, dance, dance.

During this time of life's transition, I found thought upon thought about dancing germinating in my mind. Time to put them to paper—time for other dancers to relate, smile, and say, "Yes, I know. That's exactly what happened to me." Writing notes on scraps of paper led to short stories and verses, which led to the writing of this book. Much of the inspiration is credited to Lynda and her students. Many of the verses reflect dance experiences with those individuals, who now provide the motivation to continue dancing. But more so, they have provided treasured memories.

My only regret is not learning ballroom dancing when I was younger. But life happens, and such opportunities were not realized or became overshadowed and hidden by the mundane, by the routines of school, military service and war, career, and family responsibilities. My advice to anyone is learn how to dance—learn how to dance today! I hope the verses in this collection will provide the inspiration you need.

Prologue

Anyone Can Dance

When I was just a boy, I attended an annual polka picnic with my family. There I would see a young man in the dance pavilion. Unable to support the weight of his own body, he lay, propped at an angle, in a wheelchair that had been placed at the edge of the dance floor, close to the stage and next to his family. The scene disheartened me. It seemed so out of place, so contrary to be where so many people, unconfined people, were enjoying themselves so very, very much, able to move without hindrance, celebrating the music. I was disheartened until I watched more closely.

The young man smiled. With every song that was played, as he watched couples gliding and twirling by him, polka after polka and waltz after waltz … he smiled. His head nodded side to side, ever so slightly, his tiny fingers tapped and strummed against his chair's armrests, and his dangling feet bounced and kicked to the beat of the band. I knew—without doubt I knew—that young man wanted to escape his chair, wanted to join the revelry by taking to the floor.

During some polkas, the musicians and dancers played off each other. Moments of exuberance, ebbing and flowing from stage to floor, and from floor to stage, carried everyone to a more sublime height of enjoyment. The band would crescendo with such drive and power that the pavilion would pulse, and the dancers would move with such speed that a breeze would flow from the floor, cooling the August air and tickling the onlookers before pouring outside onto the grounds. Trumpets would blare the tunes' refrains, and the snare drum would be banged with much more gusto on the accents of the ending measures. The dancers would hop higher and stamp their feet with more enthusiasm, would yip and hoot louder, sensing the songs' climatic closes, back and forth, beat after beat, back and forth. At such times the young man's body would spasm in delight against his restraints, sometimes so wildly that I thought his chair would topple. He was dancing; he was dancing!

My years of adolescence passed, each marked by their summer's polka picnic on the pavilion's grounds. After my senior year of high school and before enlisting in the army, I attended my last such gathering. Again, couples glided and twirled as polka after polka and waltz after waltz were played. The same young man's family sat in the same place it had occupied so many times before – at the edge of the dance floor, close to the stage, next to the wheelchair … this time, an empty wheelchair.

One could not miss it nor overlook it—not without reason for contemplation and past images appearing before the mind's eye—all evoked by that chair's stark and screaming presence.

But there it was, that empty wheelchair, perhaps the fulfillment of a last request, a symbol of a life lived, an act of remembrance … or maybe a message from the young man telling all, "Keep on dancing everybody. It's okay. I had a great time!"

I had always been saddened by the young man's circumstance … his unfortunate station in life. And while looking at his empty chair, I felt that same sadness again … but only for a moment because I too had reason for thought, and past images did appear before my mind's eye, evoked by his abandoned place. I remembered … and then I smiled. Yes, I smiled because I knew that young man was indeed okay. I knew that somewhere and somehow … he was dancing.

Part 1

Let There Be Dance

Ponderment

Is music the reason for dance ... or is dance the reason for music?
What a delightful ... *ponderment.*

Two Worlds

In a world of dance, couples take to the floor
where there is touching and moving.

> In a *danceless* world, there are those who sit
> and watch, perhaps wanting to be closer.

The dancers feel the music, hold frame and
step, move freely, they smile and enjoy.

> The others hear the music, tap feet, and drum
> fingers, perhaps wanting to enjoy.

Dancers celebrate the music and one another—
they waltz and foxtrot, swing and rumba.

> Nondancers hesitate, perhaps wanting to learn
> such dances but remain unmoved.

Dancers, too, once hesitated but crossed over
and now know the joys of a world of dance.

> Those who could dance, don't know and may
> always wonder … what if.

So dancers take the *danceless* by the hand, guide them
onto the floor, where their what-ifs can be satisfied …
where a choice can be made between … *two worlds.*

The Dance Floor

Where age is never a factor and abilities vary,

Where all are admitted and permission is not needed,

Where one direction exists, counterclockwise,
and doubt is to be avoided,

Where inhibitions are prohibited and under
the influence ... of music is the rule.

Welcome to ... *the dance floor*!

Choosing Wisely

On the brink of decision ... at the edge of the floor ... take that last step of a *danceless* life and fall into the enchanting embrace of the music, now set free to enjoy ... to dance.

At Its Mercy

It's the music—feel its power—obey its command.

Step onto the floor—be transformed.

Now, *at its mercy*, dance!

Part 2

Dancing

Elation

Dance with me—let the joy begin.

The Dance Teacher

(Inspired by my teacher, Lynda McPhail)

"5, 6, 7, 8."

The teacher watches and scrutinizes her students as they move to the new step, some with success and some without.

"Okay, let's try it again, this time without looking down."

The students repeat the step, and the teacher moves to assist those in need, adjusting and fine-tuning, and when necessary, switching genders in a heartbeat.

"5, 6, 7, 8."

She assesses and corrects, cajoles and comforts them. She knows when to guide or push, when to ask or demand, when to smile … and when to glare.

"Head up, shoulders back, show me proper frame."

She encourages and challenges, inspires and empowers them. She knows when to protect her students and when to let them fly … knows when they are ready, even before they know.

"5, 6, 7, 8."

The teacher is patient … ever so patient. She is an analyst, body technician, and choreographer; a leader, a guide … and friend, and at times … a miracle worker.

"Ladies, move to your left, to a new leader."

The driven students try their best, some living up to her motto, "Practice with purpose, dance with passion." And the teacher is always ready and always there, making room … for a time to dance.

"5, 6, 7, 8."

She teaches because she loves the art, the music … the *dance*. She *is* an artist, *becomes* the music … *lives to dance.*

"Okay, this time with music … ready … 5, 6, 7, 8 …"

The teacher smiles and nods with satisfaction, pride, and joy, as her students take to the floor … as her demonstrations and words become musical movement … as they dance.

"5, 6, 7, 8."

They are hers, and *Lynda* is theirs … their *dance teacher.*

"5, 6, 7, 8."

Frame

The man, the leader, holds his frame firm and sure.
The lady, the follower, enters and becomes the
beautiful picture that he presents.
They dance, she in his *frame*.

Swing

Formality ends for a few minutes as the full sound of electrified music erupts, roaring and pulsing through the dance hall.

Unable to resist, dancers jump from their seats, shuffling and hopping, hand in hand, and already in time, they hurry to the floor. *Triple step, triple step, rock step ...*

The pounding of drums and crashing of cymbals, a thumping bass, provide the undertone, the rhythm that drives the dancers.

Crazy lyrics and nonsensical syllables shouted through mics, and screaming guitars shredding the air, excite the moment. *Triple step, triple step, rock step ...*

Solos from groaning saxophones grovel in the dancers' ears, competing for the lead with blaring brass that pierces the air.

The louder the better—bodies bounce and bend, the nastier the better—bodies shimmy and shake ... just get out there and move. *Triple step, triple step, rock step ...*

Dancers let loose; single-time to the big-band jitterbugs of the war years and the frenzied rock 'n' roll of the fifties, they style to classics with East or West Coast tempos, or they grind to the wail of battered blues as it still oozes from dimly lit bars.

Bodies shift and sway, gyrate and twist as couples feel the music, their faces react to and express it—the dancers *groove* to the sound ... this whole experience, their untamed romps through musical mania. *Triple step, triple step, rock step ...*

The music ascends as the instruments and voices soar, reaching for and claiming space in the dancers' hearts and heads.

Reaching its release, the music collides with joy … but survives and struggles for one final burst of energy and readies for fulfillment. *Triple step, triple step, rock step …*

One last spin or turn, a throw and catch, then … then everything collapses … spent. The last crash of notes echoes across the floor, mixing with wows, hand clapping and laughs.

Dancers hug … then separate to catch their breaths, drained but thrilled. Play another, one more time … oh yes—play one more … *swing.*

Dance Heat, the Rumba

Slow ... quick quick slow ... quick quick slow ...

The sensual roll of a Latin rhythm lures dancers to the floor, where gliding feet join with lyrics of love and desire.

A sultry trumpet and hushed voice entice couples as their swaying bodies brush through walks and circle, ever and ever closer.

Slow ... quick quick slow ... quick quick slow ...

Only percussion and bass pulse, sealing the dancers' fate—there can be no escape as bodies touch and eyes stare.

The voice returns ... moaning as arms and thighs press with more urgency, the torrid seduction now complete.

Slow ... quick quick slow ... quick quick slow ...

The muted trumpet follows, bending its notes—hands wander, and impassioned minds envision scenes best left to imaginations.

The dancers embrace the song ... and themselves, not wanting the dance to end ... not wanting to release each other.

Slow ... quick quick slow ... quick quick slow ...

The song fades … the dance ends … and the lovers leave the floor, but arms still enwrapped and hearts racing.

With desires heightened the dancers want … need to be alone. The dance's rhythmic spell holds and passion awaits … a smoldering *dance heat.*

Slow … quick quick slow … the rumba … slow …
quick quick slow … the rumba …

That Special Lady

She has danced for years—I, for mere months. She knows I'm a beginner. I've watched her, this lovely dancer.

She asks me to dance. I hesitate, but accept ... and become anxious. I struggle, I apologize, I worry—she smiles and encourages. She tells me, "I can feel the music in you. Don't stop dancing."

We attend many dances—I falter and miss-step. Again she smiles, suggests, and assures, and watches me grow.

"You're improving ... and already a good leader," she says. I thank her for her kindness, her compliments, and patience.

We attend more dances, and my confidence grows. *I ask her* to dance, this gorgeous dancer—this beautiful lady accepts.

I lead her through the dance. She nods and smiles ... she enjoys. The dance ends, and I sigh with relief. "That was wonderful," she says.

We ask each other to dance, and we accept. "I look forward to our dances," she says. "Always dance with me."

Now I know her well and always dance with her. I tell her I look forward to a waltz and cha-cha with her ... and more. We feel the music and share the dances ... this *special lady* and I.

It's Still the Foxtrot

From the silver screens of their youth, couples recall Fred and Ginger, tuxedos with tails and stiff collars, high heels and chiffon dresses with flowing butterfly sleeves.

Elegance floated across the floor, regal and effortless; the dance world's royalty was on display.

Classic tunes became favorites, sophisticated songs crooned by Frank and Dean charmed, and instrumental melodies from Glenn and Artie delighted.

Refined yet simple, dramatic yet real, this beautiful dance and its music endured the test of time.

The couples, now more mature but youthful with their memories, still dance, less formal now, with coats removed and ties unknotted, with simpler dresses and shoes for comfort.

With smooth steps they glide, dignified and polished—a dance world's tradition is on display.

She wears her "String of Pearls" and they "Begin the Beguine." Then, and "Just in Time," he holds her hand and speaks, "It's 'The Way You Look Tonight,' my dear … *lovely*."

Later, she takes his hand and says, "'Come Fly with Me,' my darling … *let's fly, let's fly away*," and leads him to the floor to enjoy a soft "Moonlight Serenade."

For generations the music and dance have remained popular and meaningful—joy and love have been stirred and linger … in an elegant and lyrical wake of music and romance.

The songs thrive … the dance thrives … *it's still the foxtrot*.

The Dancers

They stepped and faltered, practiced and progressed—they danced.

They wondered and worried, adjusted and protected—still they danced.

They struggled and learned, shared and succeeded—and they danced.

They gave and received, laughed and cried—of course they danced.

One teacher and her students had come together—in dance ... and in life.

Their friendships and passions thrived, and they rejoiced—oh yes, they danced.

Now bound by music, friendship, desire, and joy, they celebrate, having earned silver wings of dance-flight.

They live and dance, they love and dance—oh how they move to the music ... the dancers.

Cha-Cha

Distinctive in appearance with Cuban motion, its walks and circles and playful chases, catch me if you can—move those hips.

Classic Latin rhythm cannot be resisted, whether slow and sultry or fast and jubilant—cha-cha-cha.

Sensual feel and presentation, a flirtatious attitude, with sexy steps, both staccato and smooth—move those hips.

An adventurous dance, in closed or open positions, in one spot or moving across the floor—cha-cha-cha.

Its style teases and tempts, now eye-to-eye with hands on hips, come hither, dance with me—*move* those hips ... the *cha-cha*!

Beauty and the Dance

The most beautiful reason for dancing ... is in your arms.

The Tango

The tango inspires …
The rhythm commands, while the melody and harmony of the bandoneon and guitar enchant.

The tango arouses …
Partners connect and converse in a close hold, bodies touch, arms caress, and hands feel.

The tango compels …
Attitude, with steps, quick and slow, sharp and smooth, in place and traversing the floor, intimate … yet open.

The tango teases …
Their dance is play … and it is real. The dancers' eyes cheat and glance … then turn away.

The tango seduces …
Expressions of romance, of passion, wanting yet resisting … while thoughts excite and bodies entwine.

The tango possesses …
Arms and legs hold the dancers, but more, it is the dance that embraces.

And when the music ends, memories delight … and haunt … it's *the tango.*

The Nightclub Two

A dance to feel and excite, with sweeping steps and smaller lilts. For yesterday's love ballads that still reign, and for today's songs that become tomorrow's classics.

For presenting a pleasant picture of appeal and simplicity ... and for privacy, getting lost in one another—the gentle swaying of romance in motion.

Invite to dance and say hello ... converse, discover someone new. Explore and learn, for coming to know the one in your arms, and then ... tender touching.

For holding closer, finding trust ... comfort and affection. For singing, first kisses, and special moments to come ... for awakening minds, bodies, and emotions.

Rekindle love's flame, gaze, and recall ... embrace and smile. To remember favorite songs and dances—to relive precious memories ... and arouse desire.

For words of love, spoken softly ... or a sensual caress and deep kiss. For your love ... your lover—for that someone always in your heart ... *the nightclub two.*

Dance World

Roll back the carpet in a living room, or clear away the patio's grill, with formality on a studio's floor or on a whim across a city's sidewalk,

Through a garden's walkway or on a cordoned concourse's tile, on a dark bar's grimy linoleum or a grand ballroom's parquet design,

Wherever there is space to move … whenever the music pulls at feet … welcome to *dance world*.

Partners

They welcome their song of inspiration and take pleasure in it. Now everything will be to the music's end.

One leads, and one follows—yet they are equal in task, complementing the other while expressing the joy of movement.

He presents her, and she creates the beauty—their every step, each touch and look, paints a story with motion.

He guides and embraces her; she trusts and surrenders to him. He is the melody ... she is the harmony. He is the rhythm and tempo ... she the grace and flow.

They feel their music, express it ... and delight in the sound as their every nuance embellishes the dance. They cherish their art and wander with it ... on the floor.

They *play* the music as much as any musician who conjures it. They *become* the music, its body and soul, its heartbeat and passion ... its vision ... its reason.

They are ... *partners*.

Three

Music,
Movement,
Man and woman—
The perfect ménàge a trois—dance.

The Quickstep

Walks and runs, tempered tuxedos with flapping tails—precise, unflinching frames. Hops and chasses, chiffon gowns blossom and blur— flowing, gorgeous pictures. Rooted in a roaring decade, its music mixed foxtrots and ragtime jazz—hurried yet refined.

Now catch your breath—inhale … exhale … inhale …

The dancers travel, a vibrant, colorful blend—the floor, a whirling, rhythmic palate. Skips and side-kicks, playful and stylish stepping—smooth and eye-catching. Flashing and dashing, exciting and entertaining … catch your breath … breathe—it's the quickstep.

Samba

A Latin rhythm, saucy with flash and crackle, endless in energy and sensual flow—still a ballroom dance with joyous hops and fast steps.

The Brazilian waltz celebrates a culture's carnival, costumes of feathers and sequins—but for ballroom's glamour ... don't let *waltz* fool you.

Just relax—let it happen!

A steady beat that has no end, and party hearts to match—stay light on your feet, be festive and quick.

Songs of joy and desire, a dance of play and release—shake and shift—move and sweat ... scorch the floor.

So just let go—feel the mood!

Streets of Rio scintillate with bouncing bodies and smooth, moist skin—bold and sexy revelry, with dash and daring.

Tamed for ballroom's art—but still glitz and glitter—formal dance floors can sparkle and dazzle just the same.

So just dance ... dance the *samba!*

Dance-Play

The music plays a lively swing, a romantic rumba, or playful cha-cha. Steps are performed just as they were taught, practiced, and perfected.

Then the dancing changes; urged on by the music, the dancers share moments of attraction and trust, motion ... and *emotion.* They separate but keep the rhythm and tempo as unexpected sequences occur—the *dance-play* has begun.

Tempted by the music and with inhibitions shed, the dancers *play*— one steps in place, carefree and joyful; the other circles, daring and alluring.

The dancers *style* with arms and hands, enhancing silhouettes and completing pictures that move; shifting hips, beckoning and enticing, holding secrets and promises.

The dancers return to hold, perhaps preceded by a leg crawl or hair sweep, locked in each other's arms and held fast by yearning eyes.

They bump and nudge—caress faces and necks, shoulders and waists, toss winks—imaginations rule.

The music breaks ... two beats and the dancers embrace and wait ... ... four beats, and they search each other's eyes ... ... eight beats and a scant inch separates parting lips.

Smiles and giggles confirm these moments; they are dancing ... they are *playing*—fun and affection but only heartbeats away from fulfillment of desires and passion.

The dancers move closer ... hold each other close ... closer ... closer, move less—words are not needed; eyes speak then close as they kiss. The music comes to its end—the dancers move from the floor, arms around waists ... and with a special memory.

The music played ... the dancers *played* ... flirtatious adventures on the floor to be continued later, perhaps a prelude to intimacy ... the *dance-play.*

Bolero, the Dance of Passion

The dancers respond to the enticing ambiance of an inviting and dimly lit floor. They dance—flowing with rise and fall, swaying ... as does the waltz.

A provocative melody describes the heat of their thoughts and wishes. They hold close—thighs brush purposely and deepest desires are aroused.

The couple's attraction is freely expressed, the most personal of emotions revealed. They dance—romantic movements, but much more than a rumba.

A seductive rhythm throbs, but more than one of dance ... a rhythm of love-making. They become one, savoring the rising passion of their love dance.

They inhale while reaching with long, smooth glides ... then exhale, with soft drops and drifts. They dance—sensual steps, but only a tempting taste of the tango.

Music and bodies ... partners and hearts ... the dance and emotions all come together, creating a smoldering delight.

They dance—as with the waltz, as with the rumba and tango—they dance. They touch and feel, they live and breathe, and fall into ... a *bolero, the dance of passion*.

The Dance Weaver

In the weaver's mind the dance unfolds. A vision of movement on a dance floor loom, and dancers as threads will form the unseen tapestry. From corner to corner and note to note, from heart and mind to frame and feet, all must come together.

Something pleasing to the eye should unfold, unique steps and sequences should surprise ... but with the basics still visible. Expressions should reflect the music, and movement interpret its story and spirit, something special and memorable.

A precise presentation is prepared. The dancers practice each step of each beat of each measure. The weaver suggests and corrects—they try and try ... and improve. The weaver demonstrates and encourages—they try and try ... and succeed.

Hours of practice and dozens of rehearsals later the sweat and frustration give way to fixed memories, will, and desire—everything *does* come together. The weaver watches, smiles, and nods ... but secretly worries ... and hopes.

The dancers are confident, but stress and nerves show. They stand at center floor, their weaver's loom, and wait. Dry mouth and sweating end with the playing of the first notes and stepping away, the weaver's threads create the art.

The dancers move confidently and smile, showing all how easy the dance is. The weaver sways at the side, dancing every step in her mind as they unfold before all. Then, the final note sounds and her dancers bow … and the weaver sighs.

An enthused audience applauds and cheers … as does the weaver. The dancers celebrate and feel a relief, well earned … and know a joy seldom felt … as does the weaver. All embrace and smile, satisfied at last, the dancers … and the *dance weaver*.

Dance-Flight, the Waltz

The waltz begins, and we move to the floor. Stepping and turning, our ready bodies hold their frames as the music lifts, as we lift ourselves … *and fly.*

Yes, we fly across the floor … yes, *across* the floor we glide, given flight by a silver three-four song. We feel the music and the breeze as we hold and sway with every rise and fall.

Our pleasure is shared—we see our eyes and smiles widen … and a blush appears. Our flight feels real, not imagined—around and around, circling the floor … *on the wings of music.*

Too soon, the song fades to its close … as does our *dance-flight.* But as it ebbs, its touch and thrill remain, already promising a fond and special memory.

With reluctance … and hand in hand … we move from the floor, the lingering rhythm and tempo, the unbridled exuberance of our *dance-flight* still in our step.

We move from the *dance* … from the *flight* … hoping and knowing there will be many, many more … *dance-flights.*

Part 3

Dances and the Heart

The Joy of Dance

A celebration with lyrics and melody, a reason for rhythm and tempo,
A picture of bliss and charm, a place of togetherness and sharing,
A story through song and dreams, a moment of motion and magic.

A gift for now and always, a memory to embrace and hold dear,
A journey of sight and sound, a flight of delight for body and mind,
A time for smiles and harmony, for romance with that special someone.

All these things ... they all are *the joy of dance*.

That Very Special Dance

Everything was just right. Everything was perfect—the music, the dance ... and especially, you!

Another Dance with You

There will always be another dance with you.

Reliving a dance memory ... hearing a special song, some beautiful moment of music that cannot be resisted, will beckon us to the floor again.

Wanting to dance ... needing to dance, a time to hold you and move as one with the music will compel us to the floor ... again and again.

But, *wanting* to hold you close ... *needing* to hold you in my arms and gaze into your eyes and say, "I love you," will promise ...

another dance with you.

They Dance

Their dance is romance in motion, a love affair pure and true. Heartened by their music, they fall in love again and again, song after song … dance after dance.

Magic Dance

The alluring affair with music occurred at their favorite dance hall, while a cherished song played—two lovers acquiesced to a delightful power. But they didn't know something more than a dance … something very special … was happening. That moment's mysterious perfection would not be realized until the dance ended.

The melody was memorable, providing sublime intoxication and a desire to dance. The rhythm and tempo were irresistible, providing a powerful feel … and a need to dance.

The dancers connected, and their eyes held each other as surely as their arms, and the music carried them to an unrivaled height of elation. With the song's ebbs and flows, and compelled by its lyrical charm, their senses swirled, and their bodies moved as one … as if making love.

When the song ended, the dancers reluctantly left the floor. They stumbled for words to describe their exhilaration and satisfaction—so little was said. Both were spent but satisfied, thrilled but calm—and they wanted more. A unique wonderment filled their minds. What magic had they just lived?

Such dances are rare, occurring when all elements; persons and place, song and dance, blend together for an exquisite experience—pure joy with a delicious flavor all its own that will never be forgotten.

Thereafter, when the same music is heard, memories of *that dance* will be recalled, bringing knowing smiles and faraway stares. Then, eyes will close and bodies will sway as their dance unfolds before their minds' eyes.

Taking to the floor again will be as irresistible as ever. As the moment replays and they dance, as reality and the surreal mingle, the dancers will know and enjoy again that which is already a treasure, that which was, and always will be … their *magic dance*.

A New Chapter, Dance

Two couples take their first steps onto the floor of ballroom dancing, beginning new musical journeys.

They dance the swing and cha-cha, new ways of sharing through lifetimes together.

They falter but continue, practicing and improving, learning the ways of this new world.

They dance the waltz and foxtrot, collecting new memories for their many tomorrows.

They step out, experiencing new friends and places, satisfying new desires and answering new challenges.

They dance the rumba, a new way of saying, "I still love you ... and always will."

Two couples enter the world of dance, and people see in their gazes that their love affair still burns brightly. They romance to music, and they write for their lives ... *a new chapter, dance.*

Dance with Me

Take my hand and hold me close.
Let the seduction begin—*dance with me.*

Our Medley of Dance, Life, and Love

Time

Dance with me through all of time, the seasons of our lives, until all ends. Dance me through the steps of our journey, its tempos and rhythms, through life's fire ... to its embers and ashes. Love me through life's fulfillment ... and those countless moments yet to come.

Reasons

Dance with me for all reasons, all the *whats* and *whys* ... and every *just because*. Dance me *only*, and for every *if, while,* and *until,* every *after* and *as long as*. Love me through what is magic and what is real ... our dreams and memories ... and promises.

Emotions

Dance with me for years and days, with every heartbeat and breath, vision and thought. Dance me with emotions, with purpose, and through play from twilight's blue to misty morn, from springs through winters. Love me with heart and mind, through hopes and fears ... smiles and tears.

Embraces

Dance with me to endless beautiful music, our passion and joy. Dance with me close and often, every *here* and *there* ... every *when* and *then* because I want you and need you in my arms. Love me and stand at my side, hand in hand ... a celebration of lives together.

Medley

Now ... dance with me; let us live our lives as one, and love me as I love you. *Now* ... hold me and never let me go through all that we dance, live, and love, enjoying our time and reasons ... our emotions and embraces, always savoring ... *our medley of dance, life, and love.*

Endless Dances

The music will change, but their *true* partners will not, lesson after lesson, song after song ... dance floor after dance floor.

They will glide through every smooth style and tempo, the foxtrot and waltz, the quickstep and tango.

They will rejoice with Latin rhythms, every rumba and cha-cha, every meringue and samba.

They will dance and be together, holding each other now and forever ... during their lives' *endless dances*.

Be My Dance

Be the sound so sweet and irresistible, the notes that shape and flow, the chords that fulfill and soothe—be my music.

Be the melody, memorable and delightful, the rhythm that lures and excites, the lyrics that speak our tale—be my song.

Be the steps welcomed and shared, the motion felt and embraced, the beauty held and desired—be my dance.

Yes, my dear, be my music and my song. But most of all … *be my dance.*

Two Dances

Anticipation

She told him, "Tonight will be special," and all day those words played with and tormented his mind … and the day continued.

He wondered what to expect. He thought he would explode but had to save all of his strength for her … and the day lingered.

He recalled romantic rumbas and passionate tangos in each other's arms, when they moved as one. That music played in his mind, but it didn't ease the anticipation … nor the desire.

He fantasized about what she would wear. He struggled to shake seductive images from his mind, to focus on anything … anything but her and her words … the evening was nearing.

He didn't remember his journey home to her … it was a blur and all he knew was sweet anticipation because, "Tonight will be special."

Entrance

The glow of candlelight seduced him into the room where she waited. She turned, and the quiet blaze of her amber tresses sparked, revealing the heat of a hidden, smoldering soul.

The sultry strains of music, a blues guitar, filled her chamber, coaxed him nearer, and echoed her words, "Tonight will be special."

Their gazes met and the lines of familiar silhouettes reassured them of trust and unspoken promises … of the passion that waited.

The scent of her intoxicating perfume wafted about him and invited him into her welcoming arms.

The Dances

Burning bodies swayed in the breeze of a blazing tempo and pleading melody.

Sustained notes and fulfilling chords were matched by kisses and embraces ... as deep as, and even more seductive than the music.

They held each other close ... with each step she felt his need ... he felt her desire. No need to worry ... to think ... "Tonight will be special."

Foreplay

Seduced by each other, their senses and the music, the second dance commenced, a symphony of sound in harmony with touch and movement.

Searching and soft kissing ... nibbling ... ... tasting—all excited the lovers and ignited inextinguishable flames of desire.

Clothing fell—more caresses ... more touches ... ... hands wandering over bodies, along smooth curves, to secret places of delight, brought gasping breaths.

Surrender

Beckoned by the bed, its intimate abandon heightened their arousal; hers, warm and wet, welcomed his, urgent and firm ... they became one.

Seconds became hours and minutes ... an eternity as desire burned and fantasies became oh so very, very real.

Exquisite pleasure ... the want and craving for more, conquered all inhibitions; nothing else mattered!

Stopping, questioning ... even hesitating, all were impossible and far, far out of mind ... and even further from reason.

Ecstasy

Words were not ... could not be spoken, but bodies purred ... ... moaned ... ... screamed!

Legs tingled, signaling the final ascent to the heights of uncontrolled ecstasy as the lovers neared their final release.

The ageless rhythms of life, love, and lust seized their bodies ... imprisoned them ... and carried their flesh to a climax of boundless joy.

Afterglow

They lay skin to skin, entwined in loving limbs, enjoying an indescribable mosaic of the most pleasant sensations, complete exhaustion ... and satisfaction.

The needs of flesh and spirit, rapture and affection, now fulfilled, began to ebb.

Together, and in love, the night had been special ... ... sleep and dreams ... ... hush ... ... shhhh.

Dance Love

This dance is special, private, and intimate. But there is so much more to what others see, wonder ... or perhaps know.

We step and hold—a silver waltz or tropical tango.

        I love her hair, a soft blur, swirling and flowing within our lyrical breeze—I am spellbound.

        I love her voice; its rhythm of words quiets, its gentle encouragement puts me at ease—I surrender.

We turn and glide—a lively samba or romantic rumba.

        I love her eyes; how they brighten with the dance, how they watch and embrace me—I cannot look away.

        I love her smile, revealing her pleasure and satisfaction—it holds me, and I rejoice.

We spin and sway, a happy swing or playful cha-cha.

        I love her touch, her hands in mine. I hold her, and she holds me ... close—she, the picture ... and I, her frame. I will never leave her arms ... never. There is happiness and comfort ... something special ... something of the heart.

We end our dance as the music fades.

All these things I truly love about this lady and all these things I truly love about our dance ... those moments of music with her and those dance moments to be.

Part 4

Dance Miscellanea

What Is Dance?

Dance is playful and dramatic, joyful and passionate, an expression of the body—its interpretation of music.

Dance is the release of one's very essence to rejoice, create, and share—how music is enjoyed.

Dance transforms the body, sharpens the mind, and sends the spirit soaring—it heals and changes lives.

Dance is celebrating song, reveling in one's self and partner, and entertaining those who watch.

Dance is why ballrooms are built, where friendships are forged … where romance is kindled.

Dance brings couples close. Held by music and arms, they desire … embrace and caress … then love.

But most of all, dance is what you make it … and what it makes of you.

Purity

Canvas and pallet, stone and chisel are not needed. Dance requires no gauge or design, no score or instrument. There is no want for pen and paper, for script and stage.

Dance is the purest of all art forms, inspired by the mind's music and imagination, expressed by the journey of a body's movement, nothing more—dance is pure.

Dance-Ability

Their first few notes grab attention, and all must stop. These quick surprises of song give way to a familiar knowing … then joy.

Anticipation mingles with recollections … then excitement builds. Satisfaction settles in as their sounds soothe and pleasure the moments.

Such songs have stood the test of time and traversed generations. While other songs, even entire genres, have come and gone, they remain.

These favorites have won places in our hearts and in the history of their art. They are the songs we hope for and want to hear … and never tire of hearing.

Such songs cannot be ignored as they reach and touch, grasp and hold us. They interrupt conversations and meals—they demand our attention.

These songs evoke memories and emotions, bring nods and smiles. They cause the most enjoyable of dances and become the most memorable.

Their names and their notes cannot be forgotten. Their melodies, lyrics, and dynamics have been deeply engrained in mind and soul.

Long after their play, these songs are recalled, sung, whistled, and hummed. Satisfaction, exhaled as they end, is replaced by the desire to hear them again.

Such songs are known as classics or standards and thus respected and revered. They endure, and their power is undiminished.

They are honored and described as sweet and exciting, beautiful and lovely. They stir the soul and move us … they are cherished.

When we dancers hear these songs, we *must* take to the floor ... *must* become part of the moment, part of the music.

When these songs fill rooms and halls, we dancers *must* dance, honoring them and their everlasting and undeniable ... *dance-ability*.

Mea Culpa, Mea Culpa, Mea Maxima Culpa

Bless me, ladies, for I have sinned. This is my first confession since taking to the dance floor, and these are my transgressions.

I have missed steps and botched routines; alarmed, jostled, and bumped into other couples; and I have violated the sacred line of dance.

While learning steps I have punctuated my shortcomings by muttering and not-so-muttering numerous *expletives* well within earshot of lovely ladies.

I have failed to rise and fall, drop and drift, to step with purpose and to display the ever-elusive Cuban motion.

I have not held the correct frame, pushed and pulled instead of guided or led, and looked at my feet.

I have forgotten names of steps, but much worse, I have forgotten the name of the lovely lady in my arms.

I have trampled tender toes and kicked shapely legs. I have elbowed graceful necks and snagged locks of hair.

I have wrenched shoulders and squeezed delicate hands. I have thrown ladies off balance and muscled them into position.

I am guilty of the ever-embarrassing and always surprising groping of forbidden flesh by, of course, misguided hands.

For these sins I am most sorry and ask your forgiveness under penalty of condemnation and loss of admittance to dance floors over the world. My dear ladies, please find it in your hearts to forgive me ... *Mea Culpa, Mea Culpa, Mea Maxima Culpa.*

Mea Culpa, Mea Culpa, Mea Maxima Culpa, Part 2

For my faults, for my most grievous faults ...

I will attend all classes regularly ... and private lessons every now and then. I will listen intently to my instructor, avoid wise-guy comments, and not corrupt new students.

I will dance with every available lady, and I will never refuse a lady's request to dance. I will understand that the rumba, bolero, and tango are dances of love and romance, seduction, and passion ... and act accordingly.

I will never whisper in a lady's ear the step I am about to attempt. I will take the blame for every mistake, the lady's or mine, the real and imagined.

I will learn the language of dance and use its terms correctly. I will not fear terms such as "twinkle," "promenade," and "cuddle," and will boldly speak them whenever necessary.

I will style with my arms, smile, and do my best to *connect* with all ladies. Furthermore, I will understand that the hammerlock in ballroom dancing is not the same as the submission hold in professional wrestling.

But most of all ...

I will never forget that the woman begins dancing with her right foot ... because ... because she is always right. And the man begins every dance with his left foot because ... well ... because he gets what's left.

I will never forget that a man's control of a woman begins on the dance floor (and at no other place and time) and ends with the last step of the dance on the dance floor (also at no other place and time).

I will never forget the immortal words, "Ginger Rogers did everything Fred Astaire did ... but she did it backwards and in high heels."

And until the end of my days ...

I will attend every scheduled dance event ... until I drop and am buried in my dance shoes. All these things shall be done as ... *my penance* ... really ... honest ... no kidding.

Epilogue

Inspirations

Sometimes the circumstances or the creative spark that lead to a story's telling are worthy of brief explanation. So to satisfy curiosity, or more so, to fulfill the reader's need to know, consider the following author notes for each verse.

***** ***** *****

"Acknowledgment": "A Time to Dance," written February 2012. Lynda's life has been tumultuous. In her forties and finding herself alone and struggling to reestablish herself, she began her own dance studio. Inspired by Ecclesiastes, she named her studio A Time to Dance.

"Prologue": "Anyone Can Dance," written May 2010.

Part 1—Let There Be Dance

"Ponderment," written November 2011. The word "ponderment" cannot be found in any dictionary. I made it up and use it as frequently as possible in my writings ... which is not appreciated by word-check capabilities of computers.

"Two Worlds," written March 2014.

"The Dance Floor," written October 2010.

"Choosing Wisely," written October 2010.

"At Its Mercy," written October 2010. These simple words reflect the power of music … and dance.

Part 2—Dancing

"Elation," written December 2013.

"The Dance Teacher," written December 2011. Inspired by dance instructor Lynda McPhail. This verse was read as a gift to Lynda at a Christmas party. Lynda cried.

"Frame," written February 2012.

"Swing," written January 2012. The first song, during my first lesson with Lynda, was "Honky Tonk, Part 1," by Bill Doggett.

"Dance Heat, the Rumba," written August 2011. Inspired by Lynda; we danced to "Straight to Number One" (as performed by the Andy Fortuna Production). In preparing for the routine I played the song for Lynda. She listened quietly and intently, and when the trumpet entered with its sultry wailing, she looked at me and smiled … and nodded. Blown away, she said, "Oh this is the one." We never looked back and created a sensual routine that was dubbed, "Get a roomba." We danced the routine at the Eastwood Mall in Niles, Ohio, in September 2011. We still do the routine frequently to the same song as well as other rumbas. We enjoy the dance and play during it. So romantic.

"The Special Lady," written February 2012. One of Lynda's students is a beautiful and happily married lady I will call Colleen. As I began social dancing, she seemed to take a special interest in me … as a dancer that is, nothing more. This verse is dedicated to her for having faith in me, encouraging me, and dancing with me.

"It's Still the Foxtrot," written February 2012.

"The Dancers," written spring 2013.

"Cha-Cha," written February 2012.

"Beauty and the Dance," written October 2010. One night my sleep was interrupted by this thought, so I reached for my pen and pad and scribbled the first notes for this verse.

"The Tango," written December 2012. Lynda and I danced our first tango, "Blue Tango" (as performed by Billie Vaughn and His Orchestra) at a local dance event in May 2010 … and nailed the performance. The onlookers knew I had been dancing for just six months and applauded loudly in appreciation as we took our bows. I glanced at Lynda, and she said, "Wow!" What a thrill. The tango is not easy for me, and Lynda knows it. I experience ups and downs with the dance, but we continue to work on this challenge and slowly improve.

"The Nightclub Two," written February 2012.

"Dance World," written February 2012. Lynda and her students have danced on blacktop parking lots, in a rutted farmer's field, in restaurant foyers, in first-grade classrooms, in hallways, and a hotel lobby … even a doctor's office.

Lynda and I were having lunch in a little Italian restaurant one afternoon. There were only two other parties, both in booths, and in the background, quiet, romantic love songs were playing. We heard a tango, so we danced around unoccupied tables.

"Partners," written autumn, 2011. Inspired by a routine danced to "Look at Little Sister" (as performed by Stevie Ray Vaughn) in September 2011.

"Three," written June 2011. Another interrupted sleep led to the scribbling of this verse's first thoughts.

"Quickstep," written February 2012.

"Samba," written March 2012.

"Dance-Play," written November 2011. Lynda and I danced a cha-cha to "Dance with Me" (as performed by Michael Bolton) at a local dance club. We moved ... we played like never before to this sensual and dramatic Latin number. She smiled and touched me; I can still see and feel her. She was beautiful ... our dance was beautiful.

"Bolero, Dance of Passion," written February 2012. After my first bolero lessons I began to understand the power of this dance, particularly with a special partner.

"The Dance Weaver," written August 2012. I've danced six routines, all choreographed by Lynda. She and the process of preparation inspired this verse.

"Dance Flight, the Waltz," written July 2011. Lynda knows I was a US Army helicopter pilot from 1969 to 1973, and she sometimes asks me to draw analogies between learning to fly and learning to dance. I will never forget the following moment for as long as I live. It occurred on May 8, 2011, at Lynda's silver waltz class. It had been a good class for me. Lynda grabbed me at its end and said, "Dance with me one more time." We danced our steps beautifully, better than ever before, and a most wonderful feeling came over me. I actually felt as though I were flying ... again. At the end of the dance I told her about my feeling. She said, "If it felt like you were set free and gliding over the floor, you were flying."

I was so grateful for this dance-flight experience that I gave this verse to Lynda as a birthday gift in 2011. So that she would never forget our beautiful experience of dance-flight, I also gave her a small ring of sterling silver wings.

For Christmas, I printed a nice copy of the verse and placed it in a silver frame. *"For Lynda, happy birthday, 2011, and thank you, thank you, thank you ... for teaching me to fly again."* She hugged me and cried.

Part 3—Dances and the Heart

"The Joy of Dance," written December 2013. This verse takes the elements of a song to a more personal and descriptive level, and how it affects the senses.

"That Very Special Dance," written November 2011. Lynda and I danced a cha-cha to "Dance with Me" (as performed by Michael Bolton) at a local dance club. It was beautiful. (Also, see "Dance Play.")

"Another Dance with You," written February 2012.

"They Dance," written January 2012.

"Magic Dance," written February 2012. I've been blessed with several magic dances, and they are indelibly marked in my mind. Lynda has been my partner for four of these special gifts and memories. Our Blue Tango, when I was just a beginner, gave me confidence in myself and absolute trust in Lynda, setting the stage for many more enjoyable dances. The first time I experienced "dance-flight" with Lynda blew me away; the wonderful feeling was so delightful and beyond gratifying. Then we danced a cha-cha, a "dance play" to Michael Bolton's "Dance with Me." And our "get a roomba" routine to "Straight to Number One," by the Andy Fortuna Production, thrilled both of us more than a couple of times.

"A New Chapter, Dance," written summer 2013. Friends I had not seen in years appeared at a group class one night and had a ball. These two couples began dancing after more than forty years of marriage.

"Dance with Me," written December 2013. The key word here is "seduction."

"Our Medley of Dance, Love, and Life," written spring 2013. Inspired by one of the most inspirational and special women in my life.

"Endless Dances," written September 2013. A couple that loves and is in love shares an endless love. Their bond can be demonstrated by their endless dance.

"Be My Dance," written for Valentine's Day, 2014.

"Two Dances," written February 2009.

"Dance Love," written in the spring of 2013. What better way to meld music and the emotion of love – describe dancing with the love of your life.

Part 4—Dance Miscellanea

"What Is Dance?" written February 2012. Ideas of previously mentioned verses reinforce this definition.

"Purity," written August 2012. If you need proof, stand and think of a song. Close your eyes and move to the sound and imagery conjured by your mind.

"Dance-Ability," written March 2012. At times it is frustrating to hear music that is less than desirable ... has less or no dance-ability. I understand different tastes for different people. However, I become frustrated when bands or disc jockeys play mediocre music, or instead of the original versions of songs, some cover version as performed by some B or unknown artist, or one that butchers the song. Furthermore, some songs, as beautiful as they may be, are for listening, not dancing. Responsible and knowledgeable bands and disc jockeys should know the differences. I suspect many are not dancers, or at least, don't understand dancers and the dance-ability of music.

"Mea Culpa, Mea Culpa, Mea Maxima Culpa," written November 2010. Many dance friends have told me they can relate to every line.

"Mea Culpa, Mea Culpa, Mea Maxima Culpa, Part 2," written November 2010.

***** ***** *****

Now that you have read and hopefully enjoyed this book. Don't wait another second. Get out there and dance!

CPSIA information can be obtained at www.ICGtesting.com
Printed in the USA
LVOW07s1601020415

433047LV00002B/419/P